Gowandale adventure

and other stories for boys

Ruth Burke

© Day One Publications 2007
First printed 2007

ISBN 978-1-84625-070-5

9 781846 250705 >

British Library Cataloguing in Publication Data available

Published by Day One Publications
Ryelands Road, Leominster, HR6 8NZ
☎ 01568 613 740 FAX 01568 611 473
email—sales@dayone.co.uk
web site—www.dayone.co.uk
North American—e-mail—sales@dayonebookstore.com
North American—web site—www.dayonebookstore.com

Illustrations by Bradley Goodwin
Designed by Bradley Goodwin and printed by Gutenberg Press, Malta

Contents

For
Suzanne, Peter, David and Kirsty,
with love.

was very pleased with himself, because he had hit on the idea of bringing in fish and chips to save Mum from having to cook after her ordeal at the dentist. Amy was getting cross, because she wanted everyone to look at her Viking project and nobody was.

Usually Mark loved fish and chips, but he didn't feel like them tonight. The family had only started eating when Dad brought up Gowan Park.

'I owe you an apology, Mark. I got out of work early this afternoon and went to have a look for myself. It looks perfectly safe. A better place for all those stunts than the street. So I'm happy enough for you to go there. But remember when you're cycling home to cross Park Road at the crossing.'

Mark nodded. 'Thanks, Dad,' he mumbled.

Mum was annoyed. 'Mark, I think you might have a bit more to say to Dad, after him taking the trouble to go and have a look and then admitting to you that he'd made a mistake.'

'Thanks, Dad,' said Mark again and he tried to sound more enthusiastic this time, but the park had already lost all its appeal. He was glad that the rest of the week was busy, and he had no opportunity to go back.

On Friday evening Dad announced, 'I've got two tickets for the Motor Show tomorrow. Do you want to come, Mark?'

Mark said nothing. He was interested in cars and he knew the show would be great, but he couldn't face a whole day alone with Dad.

'Sorry,' he said at last. 'Chris's dad said he'd take us fishing.' He couldn't help noticing how hurt Dad looked.

Amy, who had been listening in, piped up, 'Why do you want to go fishing with Chris? Last time his uncle spent the whole day moaning at you two for making too much noise. I'll come with you, Daddy.'

Mark slept badly on Friday night. Chris had warned him to be ready early on Saturday morning if he wanted to go on the fishing trip. There was no one about as he set off, carrying his fishing rod. At Chris's house all the curtains were still shut. Mark went round the back. Funny, the jeep wasn't on the drive. Chris was sitting dejectedly on the back doorstep. He didn't even lift his head when Mark came round the corner.

'What's up?' asked Mark.

'Uncle Sam didn't want to take us. My dad didn't even try to persuade him. I hate them both.'

Mark sat down beside Chris. He felt angry and disappointed. What were they going to do now? After a while it became clear that Chris intended to sulk for the rest of the day. 'I'm off,' said Mark.

It wasn't until he was almost home that Mark remembered that he could have been at the Motor Show. He started to jog. If Dad hadn't left yet maybe he could still go, or maybe Amy would even give up her place for him. Too late! There was Dad's car pulling out at the junction up ahead. He could see Amy in the front seat. She would be chattering away, all excited. What did she know about Motor Shows? He kicked a stone into the gutter and straggled home.

Mum was very sympathetic, but Mark didn't want her sympathy, or her suggestions. He didn't even reply when she called upstairs after him, 'Why don't you and Chris go to the new park? I could make you up a nice lunch.'

He flopped down on his unmade bed and stared up at the ceiling. 'Stupid Uncle Sam! Stupid Amy! A whole Saturday ruined.'

His Bible, with his reading notes tucked inside them, lay on his bedside table. He hadn't read them since Tuesday. Maybe he would feel better if he did. He looked up Wednesday's reading— Psalm 66. Mechanically he read down to verse 18:

If I had cherished sin in my heart,
the Lord would not have listened.

'Not much point in that, then,' he thought to
himself. 'God's not going to listen to me—unless I
own up. But I don't want to do that: I'd be in so
much trouble.'

He wondered whether he was still a Christian.
Chris was right about that, at least. Once you
trusted Jesus as your Saviour, God did 'book you
a place in Heaven'. He knew you couldn't earn a
place there by 'being good', so he reckoned you
couldn't lose it by 'being bad'. Only, it didn't seem
like a very good way of showing Jesus that you
loved him. It didn't make you feel too good inside,
either, and it was horrid not being able to talk to
God—or Dad.

He tossed the Bible aside. 'Oh, come on, Mark,'
he said to himself. 'As Chris says, this isn't
"exactly major". You disobeyed Dad once—just
once. Now Dad has admitted it was a silly rule in
the first place. He'll never find out. Get over it.'

What he needed was something to take his
mind off things. His eye fell on a box in the corner.
It was an old shoebox which had been covered
with pictures of cars cut from magazines. Mark
had made it years ago. Inside was his collection of

toy cars. It had been ages since he had looked at them, but he took them out now, one by one, and examined them carefully. There was the MG Dad had bought for him the first time they had gone together to the Motor Show. 'I could have been there today,' he thought again.

Mark would not have been too pleased if he could have heard Mum talking to Granny on the phone later in the afternoon. 'Poor Mark. He's spent the whole day up in his room, playing with toy cars. He has them lined up all over the floor the way he used to do when he was little.'

He certainly wasn't too pleased with Amy when she came home with a newly acquired expertise on cars, bursting to tell him all about every single one she had seen.

Dad was sorry about what had happened to Mark. After dinner, he offered to cycle over to the new park with him. Mark hesitated. He couldn't go there with Dad. Dad would be sure to find out that he had been there before.

'Maybe that would be the best thing that could happen,' he thought, but he said, 'I'd rather just go on our old route.'

Dad looked slightly puzzled, but he agreed, and they set off. Mark was glad to be out with Dad again, and when you're cycling you don't have to talk much. It was beginning to get dark as they arrived home.

'Look, Dad!' exclaimed Mark. 'There's a police car at our house.'

'Might not be for us,' said Dad, but Mum opened the front door as soon as they reached the gate and beckoned to them to come inside quickly. Two policemen—one very young and the other a lot older—were sitting in the front room. They wanted to speak to Mark.

'Don't worry, son,' began the older policeman, whose name was Sergeant Martin. 'You're not in any trouble. It's your friend, Chris, we're worried about. As far as we know, he's not in any trouble either, but his mum's up the walls about him. He went away at eleven o'clock this morning, and she hasn't seen him since. She told us you were a friend of his, and we were wondering if you might have any idea where he could be. Sometimes friends know those sorts of things.'

In a flash Mark saw the old carpet slung over the bush in Gowandale. 'That's my den,' Chris had said. That's where he would be. Mark looked down at his feet. He could feel a red flush creeping over his face from the neck up.

'Come on,' said the younger policeman. He was

PC Burrows. 'If you know anything, you're obliged to tell us.'

Mark glanced up at Dad.

'Perhaps it would be better if we spoke to the lad alone,' suggested PC Burrows.

Mark felt himself getting even redder, with indignation this time. They couldn't send his dad out of his own sitting room! 'I think he could be in Gowandale,' he mumbled.

'Speak up, son. You've nothing to be scared of,' said Sergeant Martin.

'If you only knew,' thought Mark, but this time he spoke out quite clearly. 'He has a den in Gowandale.'

There were more questions. 'Could you show us this den?' 'Has he just told you about it or have you been there?'

This was it! 'I've been there,' he admitted.

Sergeant Martin sprang into action. He was talking to Dad. 'Right, if this lad has a den in Gowandale, that's probably where he is. It will soon be dark and Gowandale is no place for a youngster to be on his own on a Saturday night. We could spend hours searching for this den, but Mark here could take us straight to it. With your permission, we'll take him over there now. Would you mind coming to collect him later? Sometimes a "runaway" isn't too pleased about the help his friends give the police, so it might be better if Chris and Mark didn't meet up tonight. Mark, you up for this?'

Behind him were Mum and Dad, no doubt discussing the whole affair and feeling cross with him. Ahead of him was Chris, all alone in Gowandale. Who knew what might be happening there? But, for the next few minutes, Mark was determined to enjoy his ride in the police car. He listened to the messages coming in on the radio and wondered whether any wicked criminals had sat where he was sitting now. Pity they didn't have on the siren and blue flashing lights!

Gowandale in the dark was very eerie, in spite of the policemen's powerful torches. Mark only knew one way to the den, so he led the policemen through the gap in the fence and down the rutted path by the stream. It seemed so much longer now than when they had been flying along on their bikes. There were some scufflings in the bushes, and Mark had the feeling that they were not quite alone. PC Burrows made some remark about it, but the sergeant just said, 'Let's concentrate on this tonight.'

It was hard to find the path through the

brambles and even harder to find the piece of old carpet that covered the entrance to Chris's den, but eventually Mark got there. Sergeant Martin lifted the corner of the carpet and looked inside. He came back to where PC Burrows was standing with Mark.

'He's in there OK,' he said. 'Huddled up in a ball and looking terrified. I'd say he'll be glad to be rescued. You stay with Chris and I'll get Mark back to his dad.'

Sergeant Martin had got his bearings. He knew how to slip down to the lower gap in the fence and get on to the main road. He asked Mark to phone his dad on his mobile and get him to meet them there. While they were waiting, he chatted to Mark.

'You did a good job tonight. We'd have had a hard time finding that den without you. But give Gowandale a miss in future. It's not a good place to be.'

Just then Dad's car drew up, and Mark hopped into the front seat. The sergeant leant over to talk to Dad. 'We found Chris, and he's all right. That's a good boy you have there. You can be proud of him.'

'Oh, I am,' replied Dad.

'I don't see how you can be,' said Mark, as they drove away.

Dad sighed. 'Well, I am, Mark. I'm proud of you just because you're my son. And you did well tonight. But I'm not too pleased about this Gowandale business. You'd better tell me all about it.'

So Mark told his dad the whole story. Dad said he was disappointed in him, and completely banned his bike for a fortnight. That hurt, but Mark knew it was fair enough. Mark said he was sorry and he meant it. It felt good to be right with Dad again.

'Don't forget to put things right with God, too,' Dad reminded him, as he went up to bed.

After praying for forgiveness, Mark caught up on all the Bible readings he had missed. Friday's was Psalm 32. He read verses 3 to 5 over twice:

When I kept silent,
    my bones wasted away
    through my groaning all day long.
For day and night
    your hand was heavy upon me;
my strength was sapped
    as in the heat of summer.
Then I acknowledged my sin to you
    and did not cover up my iniquity.
I said, 'I will confess

Harry's holiday

Mum tapped at Mark's bedroom door and put her head round to see what he was doing. The first thing she noticed was a large pile of neatly folded clothes lying on the floor. 'When are you going to put away those clean clothes?' she asked. 'I ironed them the day before yesterday.' She lifted the pile onto the bed. 'I thought you were going over to Harry's house. You can't still be doing homework?'

Mark mumbled something and shuffled the books on his desk around. Mum came over to have a closer look. She couldn't believe the teacher had given the class such a long geography exercise for homework. 'Did everyone have this to do?' she asked suspiciously.

Mark tried mumbling again, but eventually he had to admit that this exercise was a punishment for forgetting to do last week's homework. Mum was cross. Mark regularly 'forgot'. She was always telling him to write things down.

'But I did write it down,' protested Mark. 'I just forgot to look at my homework diary.'

Mum sighed. 'Well, if you don't go to Harry's soon he'll think you forgot that you promised to come.'

'He'll not be worried. Anyway, this is the last question and it will only take five minutes to cycle over there.'

Mum went back downstairs. 'Don't forget your helmet, and be careful: that road is so narrow at the Clarkes' house, and the traffic goes so fast,' she called over her shoulder.

As Mark had predicted, Harry was not sitting waiting for him. He was expecting Mark, since they had arranged to meet up to work together on their study on the life of Joseph for Bible Class, but he was actually on his way to the shower when Mark arrived. Somehow he had never quite got there since the football practice that afternoon. As soon as he had arrived home there had been a row with his two younger sisters, and then, when they had gone out with his parents after dinner, he had thought he might as well make the most of having the place—and especially the television—to himself.

'Make yourself comfortable,' he said, tossing Mark the remote. 'I won't be long.'

Mark flicked through the TV channels, but there was nothing to interest him, so he turned his attention to the magazines lying on the table instead. Among the Disney and pony magazines was a brochure which interested him very much. 'Adventure Holidays' it said on the front, and inside were photos of people canoeing and abseiling. He must ask Harry about that. Just then the phone rang. Mark stepped out into the hall. He could tell by the sound of the water running in the bathroom that Harry was still in the shower, so he answered the phone himself.

'Hello,' said a man's voice. 'Am I speaking to Mr Clarke?'

'I'm very sorry,' replied Mark in his best telephone voice, 'Mr Clarke is not at home at the moment. Perhaps I could take a message.'

'I would be grateful if you could. We saw Mr Clarke's advert in this evening's paper. He's selling his caravan and we're very interested in buying it. The only problem is that we're only here for one night. Could I give you the number of the guesthouse where we're staying, and maybe Mr Clarke could contact me as soon as he comes home?'

Mark assured the caller that that would be no problem. He lifted a coloured pencil from the table and scrawled down the number on the bottom of one of the girls' magazines.

'You won't forget to pass on the message?'

'I won't forget,' promised Mark. He put down the phone and started to look through the holiday brochure again. He was still looking at it when Harry eventually came out of the shower.

Harry poured them each a glass of Coke. 'Doesn't that look like a fantastic holiday? You stay in these chalets and then every day you can choose what activity you want to do—rock-climbing, canoeing, archery, mountain-biking—the lot. And the girls can go off swimming or pony-trekking or whatever, and I'll hardly need to see them for a whole week.'

This was said with so much feeling that Mark guessed Harry must have had another argument with his sisters. His own younger sister, Amy, got on his nerves sometimes, but Harry was never done complaining about Emma and Sarah. Maybe it was because they were so much younger than him or maybe it was because there were two of them and so they either ganged up on their brother, or spent the time squabbling with one another.

Harry couldn't stop talking about the adventure holiday. Mark liked the sound of it too. 'Are you definitely going?' he asked.

'Almost definitely. Though I think it's very expensive. Help, there's Dad's car. They're back and we haven't even started on Joseph.'

By the time Mr and Mrs Clarke walked into the living room Mark and Harry were sitting together at the table with their Bibles open at

Genesis and their notebooks ready. Half an hour later it was time for Mark to go home. He jumped on his bike and cycled off, wondering what plans his own family was making for the summer holidays. He forgot all about the phone call for Mr Clarke and he was totally unaware that there was another fuss before bedtime in the Clarke household when Emma discovered that someone had scribbled on her new magazine.

Harry and Mark had been seeing a lot of each other recently. It all began when Dave, their Bible Class leader, had decided to pair off everyone in the group to work together on the life of a Bible character. Later each pair was to take turns at telling the rest of the group what they had discovered.

One Saturday afternoon in March Mark called for Harry. As he turned in at the Clarkes' gate he could see that Harry was cutting the grass in the front garden and he could tell from the way that he was going about it that he was not in a good mood. 'Hardly surprising,' thought Mark. It was his job to cut the grass at home too, and the first cut of the year was always the worst. Besides, Harry had much more grass to cut than he had. The Clarkes' back garden was long and narrow, and the front garden was much the same size.

'Hi, Harry. How are you?'

Harry didn't answer.

Mark tried again. 'I was going to ask you to go somewhere with me. But I can see you're busy. I'll give you a hand, if you like.'

Harry shrugged. 'Whatever.'

Time for the direct approach, decided Mark. 'Is it the grass or the sisters?'

'Neither,' snapped Harry. 'It's the holiday.'

That was bad. 'Aren't you going now?' asked Mark.

'Unlikely. Not unless there's a change very soon. We haven't booked yet, and there are only a few chalets left for the week Dad's off work. So it looks like another year in the caravan with Emma and Sarah jumping all over me. Stupid caravan! It's too small for us now, and we wanted to sell it to raise the money for this holiday, but no one seems to want to buy it … What's wrong with you? Why are you looking like that?'

It was too late for Mark to pretend there was nothing wrong, even if he had wanted to. His face had given him away. He had to tell Harry about the man who had been 'very interested' in buying the caravan. 'I'm really sorry, Harry. I totally forgot,' he finished limply.

'Thanks a lot,' said Harry bitterly. 'You've just cost me the best holiday of my life. Yeah, thanks a lot.' He unhooked the grassbox and went round to the back garden to empty it, although it was nowhere near full. Mark took this as his cue to leave.

Mum was ironing when he got home. Dad had taken Amy to the swimming pool. Mum wanted to know what was wrong, and Mark told her all about it.

'Oh, Mark, I told you all your forgetting was going to get you into trouble. Poor Harry. No wonder he's upset with you. You'll have to go round there and apologize to Mr and Mrs Clarke, too.'

Mark turned white. 'What will they say?'

'I don't know, but it has to be done. Sooner, rather than later.'

'Sooner' was straight after dinner. Mark wheeled his bike slowly up to the Clarkes' front door. For once he was glad that the garden path was a long one. Sarah answered the door and showed him into the kitchen, where Mr and Mrs Clarke were drinking tea at the table.

'Sit down, Mark,' offered Mr Clarke in a friendly enough way, but Mark preferred to stand until he had finished the speech he had prepared. After that his legs felt wobbly and he was happy enough to sit down.

Mrs Clarke spoke first. 'We appreciate you coming round to apologize, Mark. That wasn't easy. We can't pretend we're not disappointed about the holiday. It would have been wonderful. And it's easy for us to believe that if you had remembered to pass on this gentleman's message then we would have sold the caravan. But of course we can't know that for sure. We have to accept things the way they have worked out.'

Mark looked at her. That seemed a very laid-back attitude. He had expected her to be angrier than that. He risked taking a glance at Mr Clarke to see if he felt the same way.

Mr Clarke smiled at him. 'You see, Mark, when we planned this holiday we prayed that if it was God's plan for us it would work out. But now that it hasn't worked out we have to believe that God has some other plan for our summer. As Christians we have to trust that God always knows what's best for us in the little things and in the big things in life. Our good ideas aren't always what God has planned for us.'

'It's hard not to feel disappointed,' interrupted Mark.

'Of course it is,' agreed Mr Clarke, 'but we have to remember that God can see a much bigger plan of things than we can. He's not out to annoy or hurt us. He loves us and only wants the very best for us.'

Mark looked doubtful. 'That holiday looked perfect for all of you.'

Mrs Clarke nodded. 'Yes, we thought God was going to give us this lovely holiday. That would have been a good gift. But often God uses experiences we find difficult to teach us important lessons that are useful to us for the rest of our lives. That's God being good to us too.'

'Maybe he wants to teach me to be more responsible,' thought Mark. Out loud he said, 'I really wish I had remembered to pass on the message.'

'Perhaps it would help to write things down,' suggested Mrs Clarke.

Mark bit his tongue and gave her a watery smile. 'Is Harry around?' he asked.

'He's around somewhere,' said Mr Clarke vaguely.

Mark took that to mean that he was at home, but didn't want to see Mark. He got up to go. On the way out he heard Mrs Clarke remark quietly, 'I think Harry may have something to learn here, too.'

If Harry could have done so, he would have avoided Mark, but his parents insisted that he go to Bible Class and Youth Group, and of course there was the Joseph project to work on. Mark racked his brains for a good way to make things up to Harry. He even asked Mum if they could take Harry on holiday with them, but she said there wasn't room. Forgetting things had never seemed like a big problem before, but now Mark really wanted to change. Inside his wardrobe door, where no one else could see it, he stuck up a sheet of paper where he wrote down the important things he was meant to do. He tried to look at it every morning.

'No black marks this week,' said his teacher one Friday afternoon. 'Things are improving.'

Things were improving with Harry, too. He never mentioned the holiday, and he seemed more friendly again.

'OK,' said Dave at the end of Bible Class one Sunday. 'You've all had long enough to get your studies finished.'

Some of the girls protested. 'We've had exams. We've had no time.'

'Harry and Mark, I know you've been working hard. Next week you can tell the rest of us what you've learnt about the life of Joseph.'

So the next week the boys presented their project to the class. They had made a graph to show the ups and downs in Joseph's life. He started high up as the favourite of his father and fell very low when the jealous brothers sold him as a slave into Egypt. Then there was the 'up' of having a good position in Potiphar's house and the 'down' of being thrown into prison because he was falsely accused. The graph ended on a high with Joseph as prime minister of Egypt, able to save the land from famine and to provide a home for his old father and all his brothers.

Dave was impressed. 'Very good,' he said. 'And now I want to know what you have learnt that could be useful in your own lives. Mark?'

'When you look at the graph,' began Mark, 'you might think that God had deserted Joseph at some of the low points. But we learnt that the low points were part of God's plan as well as the high points. God had a big plan. Even the brothers trying to kill Joseph couldn't interfere with that plan. At the end of his life Joseph said to them, "You intended to harm me, but God intended it for good."'

'And what does that mean for us today?' Dave wanted to know.

'Even when things go wrong, and we don't get what we want, it doesn't mean God doesn't care about us any more. We have to believe that he knows best and trust his plan for our lives.'

Dave turned to Harry. 'What have you learnt?' he asked.

Mark hoped Harry would be able to think of something to say, as he had already covered most of what they had prepared together.

Harry took a deep breath. 'I've learnt a whole lot,' he said. 'First of all, like Mark said, we have to trust God when things don't work out the way we want them to, instead of getting cross about it. I'm trying to do that. Then there was the part where the cupbearer forgot to put in a word to Pharaoh about how decent Joseph was, and so Joseph had to spend another two years in prison. I think I would have spent the whole time thinking, "If it hadn't been for that cupbearer, I'd have been out of here by now." But Joseph didn't waste his time on that.'

He glanced over at Mark, and Mark felt his cheeks glowing.

'Anything else?' asked Dave.

This time it was Harry who went red. 'Well, yes, there was something else. Joseph's brothers were rotten to him. They planned to kill him and then they sold him as a slave. But he forgave them. As some of you probably know, I have two little sisters and we sometimes fight a little ...'

A ripple of laughter went round the room. Everyone knew about Harry and his little sisters.

'... Well, maybe they're not that bad, and maybe I could be more patient.' He looked down at his feet. Perhaps he had said too much.

Dave was very pleased. 'This is exactly what I hoped would happen. When we read the Bible it should speak to us and help us to change the way we live.'

After that, any awkwardness between the boys disappeared. Mark called at Harry's house the next Saturday. The lawnmower was out again, but Harry was chasing Sarah and Emma round the garden. 'What have they done now?' wondered Mark and then he realized that the girls were shrieking with laughter, and it was a game.

Harry ran over, panting.

'Do you have to finish cutting the grass?' asked Mark.

'This could be the last time I'll ever have to cut all this grass,' said Harry mysteriously.

Sarah ran up. 'Guess why?' she said.

Emma was bouncing up and down. 'They're going to build a wall!' she shouted.

Mark looked at them all. Harry kept glancing over his shoulder at the front door. Something exciting was happening, or was about to happen, but Mark had no idea what. At that very moment Mrs Clarke appeared at the door and gave Harry the thumbs-up sign. He jumped round in circles, punching the air. Mrs Clarke was nearly as excited. She ran down the path and hugged the two girls at once. 'We're going on our adventure holiday after all,' she said.

Mark stared at Harry in astonishment. 'How come?' he asked.

Harry calmed down long enough to explain. 'The Council has been talking about widening the road outside our house for years, because it's too narrow. This morning we had a letter to say that they're going to cut a few metres off our front garden and build us a new wall. So, less grass to cut, and—the best bit of all—they pay us for losing some of our garden. Now we have enough money for the holiday. Mum's just phoned up to see if there was a space left, and there was!'

'But you haven't heard the very best thing yet,' said Mrs Clarke, and she looked as if she was about to jump up and down too. 'There was only one chalet left, and it has six beds. I was on the phone with your mum and she says you can come with us—if you'd like to.'

Harry punched the air again. He caught hold of Emma under the arms and twirled her round and round.

'I'd love to,' said Mark. 'Wow!' he thought. 'God makes some wonderful plans.'

Teamwork

Mum had once warned Mark not to listen in to other people's conversations. 'You might hear something you wish you hadn't,' she had said. Now Mark was beginning to think she was right. Not that he had meant to listen in to this conversation. Things had just worked out that way. The rest of the class was already out on the playing field, but he had been delayed because he had been rummaging around in his sports bag looking for two matching socks. In the end he had given up and was now wearing one blue and one white. As he bent down to do up his trainers, he had heard someone come back into the changing room and confront the PE teacher.

'Mr Knox, why have you dropped Sam from our relay team?'

It was Stephen and he sounded annoyed.

'For a very good reason. Sam isn't here. If he decides to go off on holiday to Spain during the two weeks when we're practising for the District Sports, then I'm afraid he loses his place.'

'But, sir,' objected Stephen. 'It was his parents who booked the holiday, and he'll be back before sports day. He's our best sprinter by miles.'

'I know that, Stephen, but the relay is a team event, and you need to practise working together

like this. Don't drop it, whatever you do. Know exactly when to start running. And don't forget to come back on Monday after school for more practice. We only have two weeks, you know.'

'I'm in the 4 x 100m relay team for the District Sports,' announced Mark as soon as he got home.

'Fantastic,' said Mum. 'You don't seem all that excited about it.'

'Of course I am,' said Mark almost crossly, but then he sat down at the kitchen table and told her all about how he had overheard Mr Knox and Stephen. 'I don't like being on a team when someone else doesn't want me there. And I'm worried about what Sam's going to say when he comes back from Spain.'

Mum understood that. 'But at the end of the day, Mr Knox is the one to choose the team and he knows a lot about how teams work. He sees you as a good team player. You could have four of the fastest sprinters on a team and they could still lose if they had never learnt to work well together. I'm sure Stephen will come round all right when he sees how dedicated you are to the team.'

'I hope so,' said Mark doubtfully.

It was turning out to be a busy month. Apart from athletics practice, teachers were starting to talk about revising for tests, and the Youth Group at church had organized a special programme. All the young people had been divided into teams. Anyone in the congregation who wanted a job done could ask one of these teams to do it for them. The Youth Group leaders thought it would be a good idea for the young people to help the older members and maybe get to know them better at the same time. And if the job was well done, donations would be gratefully received towards the Youth Group's project. They were collecting money for street children in Colombia.

The phone rang early on Saturday morning. At least, Mark thought it was early: it woke him up. Amy barged into his bedroom to tell him that Adam was on the phone and wanted to speak to him. Mark heaved himself out of bed. Adam was one of the leaders at Youth Group. What could he want at this time in the morning?

'Hello, Mark,' came Adam's cheery voice. I'm just phoning round everyone in our work team to see how you're all fixed. We have a job for today. Have you anything planned?'

'Don't think so,' said Mark foggily.

'Great, I'll pick you up in half an hour, then.'

Exactly half an hour later Adam arrived. Chris was in the front seat of his car. Mark squeezed into the back beside Harry and Philip and a huge watering can which Philip had brought with him. Mark wanted to tell Philip to shove up a bit, but Philip had learning difficulties, so he didn't. He was never quite sure what to say to Philip.

'That's our team complete,' said Adam, starting up the engine.

'Where are we going?' asked Mark.

'You promised to tell us when we were all here,' reminded Chris.

'We're all here now. We're all here now,' said Philip excitedly.

'Our mission,' said Adam mysteriously, 'is to conquer a wild jungle.'

'Whose garden do we have to tidy?' asked Chris. He sounded less than excited.

'Mrs Davidson's.'

Everyone looked blank.

'You know, second row from the back. Blue coat, cream hat. We're going to tidy up a lady's garden, Philip.'

Philip bounced up and down. The watering can bounced up and down too. 'I wish he'd move over a bit,' thought Mark again.

Without her blue coat and cream hat, Mrs Davidson looked completely different. For a start, she was a lot younger than Mark had always imagined. To everyone's amazement, she knew Mark and Philip and Harry by name. She had never met Chris before, but she wanted to know all about him. 'Chris,' she said. 'I'll remember you too.'

Adam's description of Mrs Davidson's garden as 'a wild jungle' had not been far off the mark. 'My husband was a keen gardener. I'm glad he can't see how badly I have neglected things. It's all got rather out of hand, and I couldn't see how I was ever going to get on top of it again. I am so grateful to you fine young people. You are a real answer to prayer.'

On the way to the tool shed Chris grinned. 'I've never been called "an answer to prayer" before.'

'I think she really meant it,' said Adam.

'Oh, I know she did. Let's get going.'

Adam smiled to himself. Mrs Davidson had certainly won Chris round.

If Mrs Davidson felt that she had neglected the garden, she certainly needed to have no worries about the tool shed. Every tool was polished and hanging in its own place.

'Right,' said Adam. 'Who knows anything about gardening?'

Mark and Harry looked at each other. 'We both cut the grass at home,' volunteered Harry.

'Please let me cut the grass. Please, please,' begged Philip.

Adam looked round at the garden. 'We need one to cut the grass, two to weed the beds, one to prune back those bushes and one to sweep the paths. Would you like to sweep, Philip?'

'Let me cut the grass, Adam. Please. I can do a good job.' Philip was not to be talked out of it.

'OK.' Harry gave in at last. 'I'll weed, but someone will have to help me. I don't know the difference between a weed and a plant.'

'I'll show you,' said Adam. 'Anyone know anything about pruning?'

Chris volunteered for that job. That left Mark to be the sweeper. 'And the wheelbarrow-pusher, the grassbox-emptier, the branch-gatherer, in fact, the general dogsbody,' he thought moodily as he watched Philip out of the corner of his eye. 'What a mess he's making!'

Philip's job was not an easy one. The grass had not been cut for weeks. Adam had shown him how to walk up and down in straight lines, but

Philip was small and the old push mower was heavy. Every so often he stopped to wipe his face, and to tell the others how hot he was and how well he felt he was doing. Adam praised him, and Chris joined in, but the others just looked at each other and rolled their eyes.

Halfway through the morning Mrs Davidson called the boys into her kitchen for something to eat and drink. They were all glad of a break, and glad of the nice cold drinks and chocolate-chip cookies waiting on the table for them. Only Philip refused to come in—not until he had finished his job.

'Never mind,' said Mrs Davidson. 'He can have something when he's finished. She put a few cookies aside on another plate for him. 'He's working so hard. You all are. My garden looks so much better already.'

Adam looked out of the kitchen window. 'I'm afraid you're not going to have the lovely bowling-green stripes Mr Davidson was so proud of.'

Suddenly there was a loud crash from the garden.

'Oh, dear,' said Mrs Davidson, and there was a slight tremble in her voice. 'Perhaps I ought to have moved the bird bath.'

It was indeed the bird bath which Philip had sent crashing to the ground. It lay on the path in three pieces.

'I'm sorry. I'm sorry,' said Philip.

'So you should be,' thought Mark.

'Don't worry,' said Mrs Davidson kindly. 'It was an accident, and I'm sure it can be easily repaired.' But Mark could tell that she was upset: the bird bath had obviously been important to her.

By lunchtime there was still work to be done on the garden. 'We could meet up on Thursday evening to finish off,' suggested Adam.

'Not Thursday. I'll not be back from the District Sports,' objected Mark.

'Well, if it suits the rest of us ...' began Chris, but Adam interrupted him.

'We're working as a team, so we'll come back next Saturday morning when we can all be there.' He gathered up the broken pieces of the bird bath. He was sure he had some strong glue at home which would stick it back together.

As they left, Mrs Davidson thanked them over and over and gave them a donation for the Colombian children. 'Don't forget to let me know how that little boy gets on. You know, the one who had the operation on his foot,' she said.

Amy was setting the table for lunch when Mark arrived home. Mum had gone away with some friends for the whole day. That felt strange. Mum was always around on Saturdays. Mark went over to the kitchen sink to wash his hands. He started to tell Amy about his morning. 'I think Adam should have let me or Harry cut the grass. I don't mean to be nasty, but you should have seen the mess Philip made.'

'But you are being nasty,' said Amy hotly. 'I'm sure he did his best. It's not his fault if he's not as good at things as other people! You complained enough when Stephen didn't want you on his team. You're just as bad!'

Dad came in the back door at that point. He had been hanging out washing on the line. 'What's all this about?' he asked as he dished out the baked beans for lunch.

'Amy thinks I'm being mean about Philip, but all I'm trying to say is that we could have had that job completely finished if … if …'

'… If Philip hadn't been on your team,' finished Dad. 'But do you think that's the right way to look at things? Isn't Philip as much part of the church as any of the rest of us? He loves Jesus and he wants to be involved as much as you do. Every Christian has some job to do and everyone's effort is valuable.'

'Doesn't it say somewhere in the Bible that we're like one big body and not everyone can be the eye because there would be no one left to be the ear?' asked Amy.

Dad smiled. 'That's right. The Corinthian Christians were arguing about which was the most worthwhile gift to have, and so Paul wrote to them, pointing out that just as a human body is made up of many different parts, each one important in its own way, so the Christian church is made up of many people each with his or her own gift. Instead of spending their time squabbling over who was most important, he wanted them to value one another and work together for Christ's cause.'

Mark and Amy chased their beans around their plates and exchanged amused glances as Dad tried to prise apart some slices of frozen bread to put in the toaster. 'It's good advice,' he went on. 'You young ones were able to be useful to Mrs Davidson this morning, but do you know what she's been doing for you for years?'

Mark and Amy shook their heads.

'She has a list of all the children born in our church and she has been praying through her list since the day they were born. Now there's a valuable work.'

Dad stopped talking and put a forkful of beans in his mouth. 'And something else,' he said. 'Sometimes we don't appreciate the job someone else is doing until we try to do it ourselves.' Everyone burst out laughing. He had been so busy with the washing that he had forgotten to heat the beans. They were stone cold!

On Thursday morning Mum called Mark an hour earlier than usual. Mark looked at his clock and wondered why. Then he remembered it was the day of the District Sports. 'The minibus will leave the school at eight o'clock sharp,' Mr Knox had warned.

Mark arrived at eight o'clock sharp, but everyone else was already there. Mark could see it was important not to be late for things, but he never could understand why some people always liked to be so early. There was only one seat left on the bus, and that was beside Stephen, who was looking rather pleased with himself. 'Wait a minute,' said Mark looking round, 'Andy's not here yet. We'd better wait.'

'Andy was up all night being sick,' Stephen informed him. 'So he can't come.'

Sam turned round from the seat in front. 'So I'm afraid you have me on the team, after all.'

The District Sports was a much bigger event than the school sports day. A confident voice over a loud speaker announced the various events, adding in lots of statistics about past winners and their schools, schools which Mark and his friends had never even heard of. In between announcements, the voice reminded the competitors of the regulations on where to go, and when to go, and of how to behave at an athletics event. Mark felt his stomach beginning to knot up. He wished Andy was there. Mark was the third to run in the relay team, and Andy was fourth. They had practised their baton change so often that it was more or less perfect every time, but he had never practised with Sam.

'Sam,' ventured Mark, 'how about a quick practice with the baton?'

Sam went on watching the senior boys' high jump. 'There's nothing to that. Anyway, I'll be called any minute now for the 100m sprint.'

Sam waiting for the starter's pistol didn't look as unbeatable as Sam back at home. Each boy here was the fastest in his school. Each one was determined to come first. They were off!

'Go for it, Sam,' yelled Mark.

'He's done it!' cheered Stephen. 'Sam won! We're a dead cert to win the relay now.'

The team's turn came at last. Mark felt the adrenalin pumping through his veins. The pistol shot rang out, and Stephen shot off. Seconds later Mark saw Josh pounding towards him. He turned and held his hand behind him. Now the baton was his! He heard it singing as he raced towards Sam. One boy to his left, neck and neck. Sam would soon sort that. Sam! What was Sam doing? He had started to run, but he was looking behind him, and where was his hand? Where did he expect Mark to put the baton? The two boys fumbled. Finally Sam had the baton and he was sprinting towards the finishing line, leaving the others far behind. A cheer went up, but Mark stood where he was, catching his breath, and wondering ...

The confident voice made an announcement. 'The winners of the junior boys' 4 x 100m relay are the Edward Cooke School. Torgrove School has been disqualified.'

'I knew it,' muttered Mark. 'Sam stepped over the line when I was passing him the baton.'

On the journey home the atmosphere in the bus was tense. Sam was happy enough. He had come first in the 100m and the 200m and second in the high jump. Overall Torgrove had done well, and Mr Knox was pleased. But Stephen was furious and, as usual, he was letting his feelings show.

'That Sam,' he complained, 'All he cares about is his individual performance. He couldn't care less about his team. Why didn't he practise the baton change with you, Mark? I heard you asking him to.'

Mark shrugged. He was disappointed, of course he was. But he was used to playing on a team. Sometimes you made mistakes. Sometimes someone else did. You just had to get used to it. It was all part and parcel of being a team.

Maybe that applied to this team too, thought Mark, as he climbed into Adam's car on Saturday morning. Philip and his watering can were there again. And the bird bath, well repaired by Adam.

Mrs Davidson was pleased to see the team back and delighted with her bird bath. She said that the birds had been missing it, and filled it up with water. This week Adam gave everyone a different job. Mark put on the leather gloves and snipped back overgrown branches with the secateurs. Philip was the dogsbody, and he was just as enthusiastic a dogsbody as he had been a grass-cutter. Mark watched as he wheeled away a barrow-load of twigs, spilling at least half of them on the way. At least he came back later to gather them up. Somehow, Mark felt more patient with him today.

The boys worked hard. At last Chris threw down his fork. 'Do you think Mrs D.'s forgotten about our drinks?' He sauntered over towards the back door, whistling loudly.

Nothing happened. Philip, suddenly realizing that he was really very hungry and thirsty, bounded down the garden, and peered in the kitchen window. 'Mrs Davidson's lying on the floor!' he shouted.

Hearing the commotion at her kitchen window, Mrs Davidson tried to pull herself up on one elbow and explain what had happened. It was hard to hear her through the glass, but it seemed that she had spilt some juice on the floor and slipped. She couldn't get up. And she was lying behind the back door, so no one could open it. Suddenly she moaned in pain. Adam took charge. 'We'll have to phone an ambulance and we'll have to open the front door. But how?'

Harry ran round the house, looking for open windows. Chris was convinced that the best thing to do was to take the back door off its hinges. Mark tapped on the window again. 'Does a neighbour have a key?' he mouthed to Mrs Davidson, but she shook her head weakly. What now?

Harry came back round the side of the house. 'The only open window is that little pane in the bathroom,' he said, and everyone looked up. What they saw made them gasp. Philip had already spotted the open window. It was just above an old coal shed, which was joined on to the house and had a steep roof, and Philip was halfway up the roof.

'Philip,' said Adam. 'Do you think that's a wise idea?'

Philip grabbed hold of the ridge tiles at the top of the roof and looked over his shoulder at the others on the ground below. 'I think it's a brilliant idea. I'm good at climbing, and I'm skinny enough to get through the window. Then I'll run downstairs and open the door.'

'Be very careful,' said Adam. What else could

he say? It was as dangerous to come back now as it was to go on.

'I go to lessons at the climbing wall, you know,' boasted Philip.

'But you have ropes there,' Mark reminded him.

Philip threw one leg over the ridge tiles so that he was sitting astride the roof. Then he bounced himself along until he reached the wall of the house. The bathroom window sill was almost a metre above him, and the open pane was at the top of the window.

'He'll never do it,' said Harry.

'Watch me!' shouted Philip, and suddenly he was standing on the window sill. Another few seconds and he was disappearing head-first through the window. There was a crash. Moments later, Philip's outline appeared behind the frosted glass of the bathroom window, holding up the two halves of a broken plant pot. 'Sorry,' he yelled.

It wasn't long until the ambulance arrived, and Mrs Davidson was taken off to hospital. She had a fractured hip, and it was several weeks before she was able to come home. Adam's team visited her. When she heard about how Philip had climbed in through her bathroom window, she put her hands over her face. 'Well, I'm glad I wasn't watching that, but I am also glad that you did it. I was praying that God would send someone to rescue me, but I had no idea there was such an agile climber in the team. I don't know who else could have done what you did, Philip.'

The day Mrs Davidson was to come home her house was full of people. Some of the ladies in the church were there to clean; others were stocking up the freezer, or arranging flowers. Of course, Adam's team was busy getting the garden into shape.

'Whose turn is it to cut the grass?' asked Adam.

'Philip can do it,' offered Mark, although he really wanted to do it himself. He wanted to see if he could produce those 'bowling-green stripes.'

'Sorry,' said Philip. 'I have something important to do.' He was standing beside the water tap filling up his enormous, green watering can.

'At long last, you're going to use that thing. I thought you only brought it to give us all less room in the car.'

Philip put his finger over the tap and squirted water at Mark. Mark rushed over and squirted him back. The way you do to one of your team.

Who believes in
angels?

Every second week Mark's class had drama with Mr Jeffrey. Mr Jeffrey was different from other teachers. He wore strange clothes and he sometimes talked about strange subjects in a strange way. But Mark looked forward to his lessons. Up until now they had had some classroom debates, acted out some sketches and written some short scenes of their own, but Mr Jeffrey had promised the class that soon they would start rehearsing for a proper play. He was just looking for the perfect play to suit their various talents.

'I hope we start on that play today,' thought Mark one Wednesday afternoon. 'And I really hope I'm chosen for a part.'

But it looked as if Mr Jeffrey was more in the mood for a debate. He perched on the edge of his desk, stuck a pencil in his curly, red hair and asked, 'Who believes in angels?'

One or two people sniggered. Stephen curled his fingers into a halo above Andy's head, and Andy made a pious face.

'Angela must,' said someone, but Angela curled up her lip as if to say she had never heard of anything so silly.

Mark felt uncomfortable. Of course he believed in angels. The Bible was full of them. Angels had appeared to all sorts of people, bringing them messages from God, or help and comfort when they needed it most. Off the top of his head, he could think of the army of angels that surrounded Elisha, of the angels who announced the birth of Jesus to Mary and to Joseph, of the heavenly choir that told the shepherds about the baby Jesus, of the angel who came to Jesus himself in the Garden of Gethsemane, of the angel who led Peter out of prison. But everyone else in the class seemed to find angels amusing. Next thing they'd all be laughing at him for believing in them. Out of the corner of his eye, Mark glanced over at Claire. Claire was in his Bible Class. He knew she believed in angels. As usual, Claire was sitting with her head down and her hair hiding her face. It was impossible to tell what she was thinking. Was she even awake?

'Someone must believe in angels,' urged Mr Jeffrey.

Christine spoke up. 'I believe good people turn into angels when they die.'

'Why do you believe that?'

'My nan told me about it. I think it's a nice idea.'

Angela made a scoffing noise. 'It takes some believing.'

'Angela,' said Mr Jeffrey, 'a debate is not an opportunity to mock other people.' Then he started to talk about something completely different.

Mark wasn't listening. He slumped behind his desk, feeling miserable. He had let God down. Why hadn't he been brave enough to speak up? And why hadn't Claire spoken up? He hoped she felt guilty too.

The class was almost over, and Mr Jeffrey was making an announcement. 'I won't see you for another two weeks, but I am going to begin rehearsals for our play next Wednesday after school. I am very close to making a decision as to which play we shall perform. It will definitely be one of those in your book, *One Act Plays for All*. My intention is to post a notice on the board, telling you which play we are doing, and who has which part. I should hope to have the notice up by Friday, so that you can have a few days to start looking over your words. Very good, my little angels, time to go.'

On the way home Mark had a horrid, tight feeling in his chest. He wanted to be alone. He had to tell God how sorry he was for failing him. Chris's chatter was getting on his nerves.

'No school today?' he called over to Mark, eying his casual clothes.

Mark wished again that he wasn't wearing these trainers. He explained about the field trip.

Steve fished in the inside pocket of his suit and held out his hand to Mark. 'Everyone needs something for a trip,' he said. 'Come over here, quick: the lights are about to change.'

Mark stepped into the road, and Steve put something into his hand. Then the lights did change, and the cars moved off. Mark returned to the safety of the pavement before looking at what Steve had given him. Ten pounds! That was a good start. He had decided last night that he was going to have a trainer fund and save as hard as he could until he had enough money to buy the trainers he really wanted. He had already been trying to think how he could raise some extra cash. On the way down the street he stopped to look in the sports shop window. He looked at the price tags too. This was going to be a long-term project!

Mark hung back when everyone was boarding the bus at the school, partly because he felt like a freak in these trainers and partly because his mind was still taken up with his trainer fund. The result was that he ended up sitting next to

Jim Parker. No one ever chose to sit next to Jim: everyone thought he was boring. At first Mark didn't even recognize him: he looked quite different without his school uniform. He was wearing a pullover that might have been his dad's, a pair of half-mast jeans and his school shoes. At least he was hardly likely to comment on Mark's new trainers! But what were they going to talk about during the journey? Mark couldn't remember ever having had a conversation with Jim.

He needn't have worried. Jim had plenty to say. He knew lots of riddles, could make witty, off-the-cuff puns and had a head full of statistics—football scores, populations, world records. He kept Mark entertained all the way to the coast and he turned out to be a good partner for the research on the sand dunes. Geography had never been Mark's strong point, but Jim seemed to be on top of it.

When the class had completed their worksheets, Miss Gilmore announced that everyone could spend some time in the nearby seaside town, as long as no one wandered off on his or her own and as long as everyone was back at the bus by three o'clock. Most of the class headed into town to look at the shops or search and stepped back to let him reach his seat.

As he made his way up the bus, Chris put out a leg to stop him. 'Why didn't you come with us? I'm sure you had a great afternoon with Jim Parker!'

'You should have seen what Jim did. He was amazing!'

'Mark, we have already waited quite long enough for you. Will you sit down!' shouted Miss Gilmore.

'I'll tell you later,' said Mark, and he wondered if his story would change the others' opinion of Jim.

'Where were you?' asked Jim.

Instead of answering, Mark tossed the white bag into Jim's lap. 'Happy birthday for Saturday.'

Jim pulled out a pair of the ten pound trainers. He looked pleased, but then his face fell. He'd thought of a few objections. 'But, Mark, you said you were saving up for something special.'

'I'm not any more. I'm not that bothered about having it now. Anyway, just thinking about how I could get it was starting to take over my life. I've more important things to think about.'

'But what about your mum?' Jim asked next. 'What will she think of you spending all your money on me?'

Mark grinned. 'Don't worry about that. If it's to do with a bargain in trainers, my mum is sure to approve.'

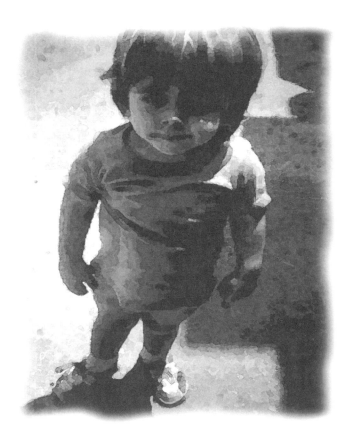

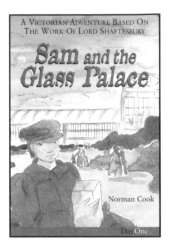

SAM AND THE GLASS PALACE

A VICTORIAN ADVENTURE BASED ON THE WORK OF LORD SHAFTESBURY

NORMAN COOK
PAPERBACK, 96PP, £4
ISBN 1 903087 42 8,
REF SAM 428

Sam Clarke is an orphan, forced to run the streets, who dearly wants an education but, above all, who needs a new mum and dad to take care of him. After coming into contact with Lord Shaftesbury and the Ragged School Union, the first part of his dream starts to come true. But will the dream turn to a nightmare when Sam's wicked uncle, Pineapple Jack, suddenly appears, or will the young shoeblack win through with the help of his friends?

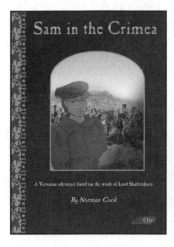

SAM IN THE CRIMEA

A VICTORIAN ADVENTURE BASED ON THE CRIMEAN WAR

NORMAN COOK PAPERBACK, 96PP, £5, ISBN 978 1 84625 045 3, REF SAMC 453

Join Sam Clarke and Carrots the donkey as they hide on board a ship bound for the Crimea... Follow them through the streets of Constantinople, where Sam and his new gypsy friends take on cutthroats and bandits. Lie low in the 'Valley of Death' as they witness the Charge of the Light Brigade and encounter Florence Nightingale. This sequel to *Sam and the Glass Palace* keeps you reading right to the end!

MYSTERY AT ARDFUAR
AND OTHER STORIES FOR GIRLS

RUTH BURKE
PAPERBACK, 96PP, £5
ISBN 978-1-84625-069-9

Meet Amy and share in her adventures with her family and friends! Why would an old lady like Aunt Roberta possibly be interesting to a young girl? What is the solution to the mysteries of Ardfuar? How do you cope when you try your best for God, and it all goes wrong?

Amy is a young girl who leads a normal life, and who, like us, finds it difficult to understand and put into practice what God says in the Bible. Learn with her the lessons that God teaches her in these four exciting stories.